MEGHAN MARKLE
Making a Difference as a Duchess

I0644094

By Katie Kawa

KidHaven PUBLISHING

People Who Make a Difference

Published in 2021 by
KidHaven Publishing, an Imprint of Greenhaven Publishing, LLC
353 3rd Avenue
Suite 255
New York, NY 10010

Designer: Deanna Paternostro
Editor: Katie Kawa

Photo credits: Cover, p. 20 Karwai Tang/WireImage/Getty Images; p. 5 Victoria Jones - WPA Pool/Getty Images; p. 7 (main) Tim P. Whitby - Pool/Getty Images; p. 7 (inset) Joseph Sohm/Shutterstock.com; p. 9 Paul Archuleta/FilmMagic/Getty Images; p. 11 Tasos Katopodis/Getty Images for WICT; p. 13 (main) Jane Barlow - WPA Pool/Getty Images; p. 13 (inset) Toby Melville - Pool/Getty Images; p. 15 (main) Brenton Geach/Gallo Images via Getty Images; p. 15 (inset) Tim Graham Photo Library via Getty Images; p. 17 Chris Jackson/Getty Images; p. 19 Samir Hussein/WireImage/Getty Images; p. 21 T.Sumaetho/Shutterstock.com.

Library of Congress Cataloging-in-Publication Data
Names: Kawa, Katie, author.
Title: Meghan Markle : making a difference as a duchess / Katie Kawa.
Description: New York : KidHaven Publishing, 2021. | Series: People who make a difference | Includes index.
Identifiers: LCCN 2020004963 (print) | LCCN 2020004964 (ebook) | ISBN 9781534534865 (library binding) | ISBN 9781534534841 (paperback) | ISBN 9781534534858 (set) | ISBN 9781534534872 (ebook)
Subjects: LCSH: Meghan, Duchess of Sussex, 1981–Juvenile literature. | Princesses–Great Britain–Biography–Juvenile literature. | Women philanthropists–Great Britain–Biography–Juvenile literature. | Television actors and actresses–United States–Biography–Juvenile literature.
Classification: LCC DA591.A45 M4455 2021 (print) | LCC DA591.A45 (ebook) | DDC 941.086092 [B]–dc23
LC record available at https://lccn.loc.gov/2020004963
LC ebook record available at https://lccn.loc.gov/2020004964

Printed in the United States of America

CPSIA compliance information: Batch #BS20K: For further information contact Greenhaven Publishing LLC, New York, New York at 1-844-317-7404.

CONTENTS

A DIFFERENT KIND OF DUCHESS

Meghan Markle's life may seem like a fairy tale. She was an American actress before meeting Prince Harry, whom she married in 2018. She then became the Duchess of Sussex and had the power to make a difference in the world as part of the British royal family.

However, Meghan wasn't just able to make a difference after marrying a prince. Throughout her life—even as a kid—she's done whatever she could to help others and to speak out about problems she saw in the world around her. Before and after becoming a duchess, Meghan has worked to make the world a better place.

In Her Words

"I am enough exactly as I am."

— "Meghan Markle: I'm More Than An 'Other,'" written for *Elle* magazine in 2015

Meghan has faced **challenges** throughout her life, but she's never let them stop her from helping others. In fact, by being open about the challenges she's faced, she's **inspired** many people around the world.

AN EARLY START

Meghan knew from an early age that no one is too young to make a difference. She was born on August 4, 1981. Her full name is actually Rachel Meghan Markle, but she goes by Meghan.

While Meghan was growing up in California, she began to see that the world didn't always treat men and women the same way. When she was 11 years old, she saw a **commercial** for soap used to wash dishes. That commercial made it seem like women were the only ones who cooked and cleaned, and Meghan didn't think that was fair. She wrote to the company that made the soap, and they changed the commercial!

In Her Words

"It was at that moment that I realized the magnitude [importance] of my actions. At the age of eleven I had created my small level of impact by standing up for equality."

— Speech given at the UN Women meeting on International Women's Day in 2015

Hillary Clinton

One of the people Meghan wrote to about the soap commercial was Hillary Clinton, who was the First Lady of the United States at the time. Meghan believed then—and still believes now—that kids can do their part to make the world fairer for all people.

FROM SCHOOL TO *SUITS*

After high school, Meghan went to college at Northwestern University in Illinois. During this time, she also worked at the U.S. **Embassy** in Buenos Aires, Argentina. Meghan finished college in 2003, and then she began working as an actress.

Meghan's most famous acting job was on the TV show *Suits*, which started in 2011. She played Rachel Zane, who eventually became a **lawyer** on the show. She was excited to play this part because Rachel was biracial, just like Meghan. Meghan's mother is African American, and her father is white. She felt it was very important to have more biracial women on TV.

In Her Words

"Some households may never have had a black person in their house as a guest, or someone biracial. Well, now there are a lot of us on your TV and in your home with you. And with *Suits* … you have Rachel Zane. I couldn't be prouder of that."

— "Meghan Markle: I'm More Than An 'Other,'" written for *Elle* magazine in 2015

Meghan's time on *Suits* was a very important part of her life. She even invited the other actors from the show to her wedding to Prince Harry!

HELPING OTHERS

Meghan lived in Canada while she worked on *Suits*. She spent time there **volunteering** at soup kitchens to feed the hungry, which she'd been doing in California since she was a teenager. Meghan also began to help people in other ways too, including working for groups that help bring clean water to countries that need it.

In 2015, Meghan began working with UN Women—the part of the **United Nations** that works for equality for women. She's given speeches and traveled around the world to help women and girls continue their education and be treated more fairly in all parts of their lives.

In Her Words

"When we empower girls hungry for education, we cultivate [grow] women who are emboldened to effect change within their communities and globally [around the world]. If that is our dream for them, then the promise of it must begin with us."

— Writing for *TIME* magazine in March 2017

Meghan proudly calls herself a feminist—someone who believes in and fights for equality between women and men. Meghan has written about being a feminist and the work she's done to help women and girls for magazines and on a website she used to run called *The Tig*.

MEGHAN AND HARRY

Meghan was hard at work acting and helping others when she met Prince Harry in 2016. They connected over their hopes to make a difference in the world, and they soon fell in love. In 2017, they announced that they were **engaged**, and on May 19, 2018, they were married in St. George's Chapel in England.

Meghan and Harry became the Duke and Duchess of Sussex after they were married, and people around the world wanted to know more about their lives. This included their lives as parents after they welcomed their son, Archie, into the world on May 6, 2019.

In Her Words

"It was one of the first things we started talking about when we met was just the different things we wanted to do in the world and how passionate [excited] we were about seeing change."

— Interview with the BBC from November 2017, speaking about her relationship with Prince Harry

As a biracial American actress, Meghan was a new kind of royal. She and Harry have inspired people by being open about their love for each other, the work they want to do to help others, and the challenges they've faced as part of a very public family.

AROUND THE WORLD

As members of the British royal family, Harry and Meghan traveled to countries around the world to represent, or stand in for, Queen Elizabeth II, who's Harry's grandmother. When they'd travel to different countries, Meghan would often meet with women to learn about their lives and what other people could do to help them.

One part of the world that's very important to both Meghan and Harry is Africa. They visited Africa together not long after they began dating, and they went back after their wedding too. When they toured Africa in 2019, they talked about helping the people who live there, especially women and children.

In Her Words

"On one personal note, may I just say that while I am here with my husband as a member of the royal family, I want you to know that for me, I am here as a mother, as a wife, as a woman, as a woman of color, and as your sister."

— Speech given in South Africa in September 2019

Africa also meant a lot to Harry's mother, Diana, who died in 1997. She spent a lot of time helping people in Africa, and many people see Harry and Meghan's work in Africa as carrying on the work she started.

Diana, Princess of Wales

COOKING FOR A CAUSE

When Meghan became a duchess, she chose causes close to her heart to officially support, which are called royal patronages. She officially supported groups that work with animals, deal with education, and help women find jobs. She supported the National Theatre too.

Meghan also worked in other ways to help women. This included writing a cookbook with a group of women whose families lived in a building in London, England, that burned down in 2017. These women then started cooking together at a place called the Hubb Community Kitchen. The money made by *Together: Our Community Cookbook* went to help those women.

In Her Words

"There is a role [part] for all of us here. As women we can listen to one another, and lift each other up; we can raise our boys to be men who value women. And for men and boys, you can lead by example and not let your mothers, daughters, sisters, wives and girlfriends ever feel that they are lesser than you."

— Speech given in South Africa in October 2019

Meghan is shown here helping out at the Hubb Community Kitchen. Meghan loves food and cooking, so helping the women who cook there was a perfect fit for her.

FACING HARD TIMES

Sometimes people can make a difference by sharing that things aren't always easy for them, which helps others feel less alone. Meghan and Harry have been very open about how hard it can be to lead a very public life. Meghan has dealt with a lot of unfair and unkind stories being written about her, and she's talked about how this has hurt her feelings.

Meghan and Harry both believe in the importance of privacy and taking care of their **mental** health. Because of this, in January 2020, they announced that they were stepping back from being **senior** members of the royal family.

In Her Words

"I have said for a long time to H—that's what I call [Harry]—it's not enough to just **survive** something, right? That's not the point of life. You've got to thrive, you've got to feel happy."

— *Harry & Meghan: An African Journey*, a **documentary** about their 2019 trip to Africa

The Life of Meghan Markle

1981
Meghan Markle is born on August 4.

2003
Meghan finishes college at Northwestern University.

2011
Meghan begins playing Rachel Zane on the TV show *Suits*.

2015
Meghan starts working with UN Women.

2016
Meghan meets Prince Harry.

2017
Harry and Meghan announce their engagement.

2018
Harry and Meghan are married on May 19.

Together: Our Community Cookbook comes out in September.

2019
Meghan and Harry's son Archie is born on May 6.

Meghan, Harry, and Archie visit Africa.

2020
Meghan and Harry announce that they're stepping back from being senior members of the royal family.

Meghan Markle has made a difference in many ways before and after she became a duchess, and she's still looking for new ways to help people in the world around her.

A NEW BEGINNING

Before and after Meghan and Harry announced their new plan for their lives, they spent time away from England, including in Canada. They wanted to raise Archie with more privacy than they would have in England. They also felt that stepping back from the world of the royal family would give them a chance to make a difference in the world in their own way.

Making a difference isn't new for Meghan Markle. She's been trying to make the world a better place since she was a kid. Her story shows us that there are many ways for one person to help others.

In Her Words

"It is said that girls with dreams become women with **vision**. May we empower each other to carry out such vision—because it isn't enough to simply talk about equality. One must believe in it. And it isn't enough to simply believe in it. One must work at it. Let us work at it. Together. Starting now."

— Speech given at the UN Women meeting on International Women's Day in 2015

Be Like Meghan Markle!

Write letters to leaders about changes you believe should be made to help the world become a fairer and more equal place.

Be proud of who you are, and remind others to be proud of who they are too.

Raise money for groups that are working to help people in your community and around the world.

Volunteer at a soup kitchen or for another cause you care about.

Treat all people with kindness and respect.

Talk openly about causes you care about and things you believe are important.

Take care of your mental health by being open with a trusted adult about problems you're dealing with, such as bullying.

It may seem like it's hard to be like a duchess, but there are plenty of ways you can be more like Meghan Markle. These are some ideas!

GLOSSARY

challenge: A problem.

commercial: A clip on television or the radio that is created to get people to buy something.

documentary: A nonfiction movie or television show presenting facts about a subject.

embassy: The building where a group of people who represent their country in another country live or work.

engaged: Promised to be married.

inspire: To move someone to do something great.

lawyer: A person whose job it is to guide and help people in matters relating to the law.

mental: Relating to the mind.

senior: Having a higher standing than other people in the same position.

survive: To keep living.

United Nations: A group formed in 1945 to help countries better work together.

vision: The ability to see and plan great things for the future.

volunteer: To do something to help because you want to do it.

FOR MORE INFORMATION

WEBSITES

Harry and Meghan: An African Journey

www.youtube.com/watch?v=j_c7ZhK0AKA

The full documentary about Harry and Meghan's visit to Africa in 2019 can be found on YouTube.

IMDb: Meghan Markle

www.imdb.com/name/nm1620783/

The Internet Movie Database features facts about Meghan's life, especially her work as an actress before becoming a duchess.

BOOKS

Felix, Rebecca. *Meghan Markle.* Minneapolis, MN: ABDO Publishing, 2019.

Golkar, Gloriz. *Meghan Markle.* North Mankato, MN: Capstone Press, 2019.

Krajnik, Elizabeth. *Meghan Markle: American Royal.* New York, NY: Enslow Publishing, 2019.

Publisher's note to educators and parents: Our editors have carefully reviewed these websites to ensure that they are suitable for students. Many websites change frequently, however, and we cannot guarantee that a site's future contents will continue to meet our high standards of quality and educational value. Be advised that students should be closely supervised whenever they access the Internet.

INDEX